CHECK OUT THE OTHER BOOKS TO THE SERIES

BOOK ONE

Life with Paranormal Encounters

BOOK TWO

Home Sweet Haunted Home.

LIFE WITH

PARANORMAL
ENCOUNTERS

BOOK III

THE WALLS THAT SCREAM

BY CONNOR BIDDLE

The Walls That Scream

-

Life with Paranormal Encounters | Book 3

PARANORMAL ENCOUNTERS

Imprinted by
Paranormal Encounters

ISBN 9780578397191

Printed in the USA

For Pam.

The one who's *always* been there since 1991.

I love you.

TABLE OF CONTENTS

TABLE OF CONTENTS

FOREWORD

anaging Whispers Estate and being part of this house for 11 years as of to this date has been nothing short of a crazy roller coaster ride. When I started coming here with my paranormal team 12-13 years ago, there was nothing in the world to prepare me or the girls I was with what was about to unfold as the night led on.

This was our second trip to this haunted Victorian house and the very first time our team was here we had gone up into the séance room where we were taking pictures in this big diamond shape mirror and I had gotten this amazing picture of what looked like a 6 year old boy with brown curly hair and you could even see the sideways strips in his shirt he had on. When we had come back this second time I thought well I will try to recreate that picture from the very first night we were here. Like I had said earlier, nothing in the world would prepare none of us that was in that room for what was about to happen.

As the hours ended for us and we were about to wrap up our investigation for the night and morning hours were now upon us. It was getting late we were tired so we were trying to decide what to do to end our time at Whisper's so, the guys of the group decided to stay in the front parlor all but one and he decided to go with us females.

We grabbed the equipment we were going to use and headed up. Arriving at the top he went into the Red Room as the four of us females went into the Séance Room directly across from him. I decided to sit on the step just as you walk into the Séance Room so I can get my pictures in the mirror to try to recreate the picture of the prior investigation and the other three women would go a little further into the room to sit.

The entire attic was darker than the abyss we all gathered around with the K-2 Meter between us. We weren't in the attic but about five minutes when I could feel something coming up the staircase to the attic behind me. Whatever this was that was coming was not good. No matter how hard I tried I could not shake this feeling that is was creeping upon us. I did not want to turn around to look so I just turned my camera around and took about three pictures and brought it down and looked but nothing was showing in the pictures. However, I could still feel this entity coming and knew it wasn't good.

All of a sudden our K-2 starts spiking to red continuously. I said, "We have spikes on our K-2" and Mary said, "Who is here with us". All of a sudden about that time it was like the room got all chaotic and it all hit simultaneously. From different directions in the room, there was a gust of wind, a loud growl, and then something right beside me on the step by where I was sitting let out this hellacious blood-curdling scream that was ear piercing. Like the scream of a Banshee!

I jumped up from the step darting forward towards the other three women because we couldn't go out the door to get out because it was like we were barricaded in the room at this moment and no way past what was screaming at us. We all ran to the far corner of the room gathering together screaming for our lives unsure of what had or was transpiring. You could not see this entity but you could just gauge it. Whatever this was it was coming for us in almost like a slow crawl screaming.

Meanwhile downstairs in the front parlor, the guys had heard a very loud thump. So loud they thought someone had fallen down the stairs so they took off to go see what had happened to see if everyone was okay but they were on the first floor and we were in the very top upstairs attic pinned in the corner by this bone-chilling unseen and unworldly force that at that moment seemed like it was going to eat us. The guys finally topped the attic stairs, as they came around the corner which seemed like forever when there is nothing but terror and you feel like you are living a horror film.

When they topped the attic steps and came around the corner of the room we were in, the screaming had abruptly come to a stop. By this time the entity was already right up in our face nose to nose. Then it was gone just like that! We were shook to our soul; all of us trembling.

We went back downstairs to gather ourselves and try to even phantom what had just had happen to us. We all discussed everything and then parted our ways all going home. However, what I didn't know was my life was about to take another turning point. Something attached or followed I don't know but then I was being held down in my bed by big dark black shadows hovering above me while another one was sitting in a chair at the foot of my bed with this wicked grin on its face. I could see my cat out of the corner of my eye sitting on the floor just staring up at it as it sucked all the breath out of me yet I couldn't move. All I could do was look around the room. The person staying with me at that time yelled out "Nooo get away from her and leave her alone" then grabbed me. The black shadows dissipated and it took a bit to catch my breath. We cleansed the home and cleansed the home but you could just tell it took a while to get them out until finally one day it was successful.

For the longest time my cat would scream and take off under the blankets or take off running through the house and it just sent total chills throughout your entire body because you knew they were near again. I stopped paranormal investigating for the longest time probably for about a good year or so and didn't want anything to do with it and was pretty sure after all that I was going to quit because well let's be honest no one wants to be eaten by something, especially something they can't see that you can only about visualize in your mind what it looks like.

One of the other girls with me Kim was over a big paranormal chapter and had been, and she got out for good. Her words "I cannot un-hear what I heard that night"! I came back to Whispers after a good while after the manager talked me into it and I have now been here for 11 years managing it myself. I am very grateful for Whispers and its experience's good and terrifying as well as having the opportunity to meet so many amazing people along the way that come into my life like Connor and India with Paranormal Encounters. Their just great down-to-earth people and having them at Whispers was great to see how they film and Investigate. What attracts me most to them specifically is their honesty in what they do. If it doesn't happen and it's not that active that specific night well then, they don't try to stretch the truth just to get coverage for the sake of their filming. Cause if you are a seasoned investigator then as we all know you do not get activity every time you go somewhere. You can go to that same place 2-3 times and nothing then on the 4th time it's crazy. That is, in fact, the way the paranormal life is and I highly respect Connor and India in which the matter they present and film as well as Connor for telling and writing through his perception and eyes.

PROLOGUE

Fiorella Damask red and yellow striped wallpaper lines around the dark wood-floored room. A crystal chandelier hangs evenly in the center of the white swirl ceiling. A piano, couch, and coffee table occupy the loneliness of this room. This, of course, is not the same original setting or furniture from this particular Thursday of Christmas Eve 1912. Much has changed, except one particular thing. The wooden pocket door is charred with burns that scatter when attention is given to this area of this room; it is the only thing that remains original and untouched.

This particular night was cold. The skies were clear and flurries of snow trickled down until morning. The moon this night illuminated areas in the house where no light was. The windows throughout had condensation from the water pipes heating the rooms where a family lived. Dr. John Gibbons, his wife Jessie, their six-month-old daughter Helen, and adopted daughter Rachael slept motionless in their beds. Not a sound could be heard, other than the drops of water running along the glass windows and onto the still. That is, however, until a blood-curling scream rushed throughout the house and echoed into John and Jessie's bedroom. Their eyes shot open and their stomachs squealed in fear as they stood up within an instant. The screaming continued. It was a child. But it wasn't just any child — it was Rachael.

The couple frantically scattered out of their bed, running towards the sound and down the wooden stairs that led to the first floor. The screaming was coming from the first room at the bottom of the steps — The Parlor. The smell of burning wood filled the air and smoke seeped out of the room. The Gibbons rushed into the scene, looked to the right side corner of The Parlor, and quickly noticed the family Christmas tree, presents, and everything around the area was engulfed in flames; including their adopted daughter Rachael. She was pinned in the doorway from the Christmas tree, screaming in agony as the fire tore through her nightgown, hair, and body. Jessie gasped as her heart sank to the bottom of her stomach in sheer panic. John cried out running to Rachael's aid, quickly pulling her from the grasp of the burning tree and dragging her towards the other side of the room to Jessie. By this time, Rachael had suffered major burns and was in critical condition.

John then rushed to the kitchen to gather buckets of water to put out the fire. The damage was already done and this moment was *burned* into the pocket door where a trail slithered along the surrounding doorways' wood frame. This is when this tragic moment was forever recorded. Rachael was eventually taken to her bedroom on the second floor where she lay in her bed in and out of consciousness, suffering from her burns, and would die three days later.

CHAPTER ONE
DEATH | PART ONE

The moment of death is instant, permanent, sudden, and without warning. It's when our internal workings stop, and our clock ceases to allow time in the living realm. Death is said to be the passage from this life to the next.

Since the beginning of our conscious mind, humans have often asked themselves, what happens next? The answer, however, is uncertainty; it remains the greatest mystery of the human existence. Ancient cultures over the centuries have developed their own ideas and illustrated them in hieroglyphics and sacred texts.

It is with this great mystery that many people turn to their religion for the answers they seek which science has failed to provide. In the modern belief, however, there are three places that popular religions have said awaits us after our final breath on Earth. Heaven, Hell, or a place called Purgatory; the process of purifying the soul by temporary suffering. Where ever this place may be that our soul ends up; the invisible force that makes up our personality — the very characteristic essence of who we are, must go somewhere, right?

There are too many strange and unexplainable cases that people have reported experiencing inside their homes. These kinds of things are called hauntings; it is the belief that spirits of the dead inhabit a location, creating unnatural events to occur. I guess one could call this the Purgatory humans must undergo if such a place like Heaven and Hell exist.

Every haunting, however, begins with a ghost story. Every ghost story begins with a haunting. The woman in white who's been said to be seen walking the hallways. The little boy who died unexpectedly from an illness is said to play with toys in a certain room. The savage murder of a couple and now they are heard throughout a home at a certain hour in the night. We must ask ourselves, what makes a place haunted? Is it death or can it be something more?

The paranormal field I find likes to use the idea that tragic events are the sole purpose for this. This is because that said person died suddenly, unexpectedly and their spirit hasn't crossed over to the afterlife due to having unfinished business with the living. The belief of those who feel this is the reason for hauntings also feel that the living can help a spirit crossover from this plane. What if we assumed the opposite and I told you that I do not feel that spirits of the deceased actually need help from the living? Let's assume that a spirit is something of supernatural elements, how would they benefit from a mortal? It sounds much more complicated than chanting some words or practicing some spell that is said to accomplish such a great feat. Logically, it does not make sense.

For those who don't know me, my name is Connor Biddle, and I am a paranormal enthusiast and documentary-style filmmaker. I started a show in the year 2012 called Paranormal

Encounters. Since then I have been to numerous places around The United States of America. I stopped filming for two years until the year 2019 when Paranormal Encounters was revamped. Instead of the show following myself and the random people who happen to just be in the videos, this time around it consisted of myself and my other half, India.

At the time of writing, my experiences in the last three years with the paranormal have been even more defining than the previous nine. I have been gifted to have plenty of ghost stories to tell that most spend a lifetime searching for. Some of which I still cannot believe to this day.

This is the third book in the Life with Paranormal Encounters series which details those experiences through my eyes and the things that were never put into the episodes. When I first began my relationship with the paranormal, I often called myself a paranormal investigator. I think this was mostly due to my obsession with the paranormal shows that were getting popular at the time and the people in these shows carried that title. I unconsciously mimicked many of their tactics and personas that it took me years to shake off and find my own purpose in the realm of the paranormal.

I have found over the years that what I do now has a different meaning than what I thought it did. I'm not a paranormal investigator; I prefer to be known as a paranormal enthusiast. The reason for this is the fact that I do not investigate claims of the paranormal at specific locations, but rather I've found myself attached to the subject matter itself.

Let me explain. I love the paranormal but I also like to challenge popular culture beliefs and seek out other possibilities for the events that I have experienced. I have always been the kind of person who refuses to follow the herd but rather finds myself veering in a different direction than my peers. Maybe it's just my ambition talking and the denial of the common practice that makes me this way. Maybe I am the black sheep of the paranormal. I constantly look back on my encounters with peculiar events that I believe were paranormal and wonder how this happened. Why did I experience this? Why are so many haunted locations I have visited associated with death? Is it something psychological or maybe my essence connects with the hidden world and I am meant to seek it out? I am obsessed with just thinking about it to where it has taken over almost everything I do on a daily bases. It seems as though from the start of my paranormal journey I have found myself asking more questions rather than finding the answers I once thought I wanted closure on. I no longer need proof that the paranormal is real. I just want to understand it more and see what experience tops the last.

I know that I can never prove what I say or do as being authentic to those who watch my show, Paranormal Encounters which documents these types of experiences, or read my books that go further into details of my encounters. I can only supply what I think and the reasoning for what makes those feelings up.

I have been to numerous places throughout The United States that are said to be highly active with paranormal activity, and I have left them all with plenty of stories to tell. However, I never did a paranormal investigation at a location where it left me speechless until I visited a three-story house in the state of Indiana. This was a moment in my paranormal journey I feel is truly rare. A glimpse of the supernatural, the kind that Hollywood likes to portray in their movies. At the time of writing this book, it has been 18 months since this encounter, and not a day goes by that I haven't had this night on my mind.

I am about to take those who have delved into this book inside one of the most terrifying houses in America. This is the story of how myself and India were given the opportunity to film an episode of our show inside the Whispers Estate.

If you are seeking a ghost story about a truly haunted house, then you've found one, or maybe it found you.

CHAPTER TWO
HOW IT HAPPENED

This all started when India and myself were seeking out locations to film for season two of Paranormal Encounters. It was towards the end of the season, our YouTube channel was quickly growing and my hunger for being inside places said to be haunted started to become irresistible.

The two of us lived in South Carolina, a state I found that was not as welcoming as I had liked in regard with allowing access to buildings that were reported to be haunted. It, unfortunately, seemed as though the majority of our filming in season two was in the state of Indiana, a ten-hour road trip both ways. This was just how it ended up because I wanted our road trips to be worth it. I worked five days of the week in retail and when it came to the time when we would film, I requested my Fridays for a three-day weekend. The purpose of that was so we could get up early in the morning, drive ten hours to our first location, film that night, wake up the next day and repeat it two more times at different locations each night before I went back to work on that coming Monday. It was tiring, but I knew we had to make this next trip worth it for our viewers.

It just so happened that the owner of two locations we filmed for our second season, Dan Allen, also owned two more locations. One was called The Liberty Township School which he was preparing to open to the public for paranormal investigations and the other was The Blackford Jail. The school was just over the border into Ohio and the jail was in Hartford City, Indiana. We had planned to film the school on a Friday and the jail on Saturday but we needed to find one more location for Sunday. Unsuspecting to us, however, these two locations would leave us almost empty-handed. And on the way to our third place to investigate, I was trying to be optimistic. It's understandable that not every place will be active, but I was really looking for that next big experience.

When I look for locations that are possibilities for filming episodes, I jot them down in a notepad to later contact. There was one location I had on the list that I have known about since I started my journey into the paranormal — The Whispers Estate.

This location took on a name for itself over the years. When I was in high school, I lived in Northern Indiana and I always saw things about this place as I was working on making a name for myself. All I really knew was that it had a reputation for people getting attacked and leaving with phantom scratch marks; this always drew my interest. I am the type of person who carries healthy skepticism with each place I travel to. I choose to do this to keep myself from subconsciously thinking it's active without irrational thinking. If someone told me something crazy about some kind of activity that is reported to happen, I would happily submerge myself into that kind of situation to see if it happens to me. I feel that this is a necessity when exploring the paranormal. If I treated it any differently, then I would have to ask myself why am I doing this in the first place?

It was on a Tuesday afternoon that I had looked to find the contact information to book our investigation at The Whispers Estate and after some searching, I ended up finding their Facebook page. I scrolled down the web page, saw a contact number, and gave it a call. The rhythmic tones echoed in my ear.

Ring.....Ring.

A man answered the phone and introduced himself as Rich Ballard. The 'Hello' in the tone of his voice carried the impression that he was a very energetic and talkative type of person. I asked if this was the right contact information for booking The Whispers Estate and Rich told me that it was and that he was the owner of the establishment. I introduced myself and told him that I had an interest in filming an episode of Paranormal Encounters at the house. He seemed open to the idea but cautious. I think Rich wanted to make sure we weren't going to make a video about anything that could damage the reputation of his newly acquired location. He had only owned The Whispers Estate for around seven months at the time I contacted him.

Over the years, before Rich took ownership of The Whispers Estate, paranormal investigators would frequently create videos about how the house was evil. This was mostly because of the numerous photos of people showing scratch marks or videos of alleged possessions. I find that most people like to associate that with something demonic; which in my experience and opinion is not. The possession part I feel is unlikely, rare, and just mere acting to receive attention.

As I spoke more with Rich over the phone he told me that the investigation cost varies by the day of the week. I told him that we were looking to do it on a Sunday and he said it would be two hundred dollars that we could pay through a website called *Eventbrite*. This is a very good price because it is extremely common for locations to charge ungodly amounts of money and for very limited access.

Rich asked to see our previous work before our filming. He would text me later that night telling me that his son watches the show and was eager to see the episode we would create. I was excited but I now felt that I had an obligation to make a good impression.

I asked Rich if we could interview him about any of the ghost stories he may know or had experienced. It was without hesitation at the end of my question that he agreed. I then asked if Rich knew anyone else we could get on camera and he told me that a woman by the name of Sondra, who caretakes the home, would be willing to talk about the history, as she had been involved with Whispers Estate for over a decade.

• ⊁≕❖❍❖❖≕⊀ •

It was August 30th, 2020 on a Sunday when we filmed our episode at this truly haunted house. I can only confirm that it is truly haunted because it takes certain things to happen for me to feel this way. There are only less than a handful of times in the past twelve years and this one is one of those.

CHAPTER THREE
WHISPERS ESTATE

The Whispers Estate is located in the heart of Mitchell, Indiana, where it sits nestled on a quiet street. Street lights line the sidewalk, and trees fill the property. It was constructed at the end of the 19th century and it shortly after fell into the hands of a doctor named John Gibbons. He lived inside the home with his wife Jessie. The couple was known for adopting unwanted children; this entailed orphaned or abandoned ones. One of these children, a 10-year-old girl named Rachael, is to this day the main focus when talking about the hauntings at the Whispers Estate.

It's a tragic story that one will find when looking up information about the home. This is the majority of what will be seen when looking for any deaths that occurred within the walls of this establishment. It was a huge story in the local newspapers. Ever since I found out about the house, I knew of there being an old story of a young girl sneaking downstairs in the middle of the night and somehow died in a fire. I was not sure of any more details but I knew it was said that her spirit has seen roaming the hallways of the Whispers Estate.

I spent zero time looking into the history and the hauntings before our filming because I wanted to hear the stories for the first time on camera. I also felt this helped in preventing myself from subconsciously thinking I experienced anything. So, one can only imagine how eager I was to hear more about this little girl.

It was nine o'clock Sunday morning. I awoke in the bed of my hotel. The exhaustion started to kick in from the two previous sleepless nights. Sleepless because I had spent the last two nights doing paranormal investigations and filming for my show Paranormal Encounters. The first thought on my mind was how I felt like India and I was on a losing streak of experiencing and capturing anything paranormal on camera. This was the third and last day of filming. The day where we were going to come face to face with Whispers Estate.

We just finished packing our things, loaded them into the trunk of my car, and made our way south. The city of Mitchell, Indiana is around a three-hour drive from The Blackford Jail. The drive wasn't anything memorable, it was mostly cornfields and small run-down towns. Oh, and lots of Take Me Home, Country Road by John Denver playing on repeat. I remember the wind that day vividly. For some reason it was absolutely terrible; my car felt like it was being pushed from side to side on the road. I kept asking myself if this was some type of omen insinuating that this location too, was going to be another failure of a night in communicating with something paranormal. I had to try and stay optimistic; I had to.

Over the years I have developed a hypothesis that every time I experienced something I believed was paranormal, it was because my mind was clear of negativity. In my opinion, I believe spirits communicate with the living telepathically not verbally, they already know our intentions; this is how we communicate.

It was around four in the afternoon, an hour later than I planned when India and I arrived in Mitchell Indiana. I had asked Rich if we could come earlier than the six o'clock start time that most people do because I wanted to fly my drone and film exterior shots before the already overcast sky got any darker. If it wasn't for the winds, however, I would have arrived earlier. But that is usually our kind of luck — bad luck.

I remember the moment we turned on the street where Whispers Estate sat. The GPS on my cellphone stated, "You have arrived." I could see The house slowly peek into view from behind the trees in the front yard.

The excitement started to rush throughout me. It's the first time seeing a location that does it to me. It's like meeting a celebrity that you've seen through pictures and videos. It's a surreal moment and a part of the paranormal that I truly love.

Whispers Estate nestles quietly on West Warren Street. It's a three-story, four-thousand square foot location with nearly nine bedrooms and a basement. Gray-colored siding, black roof, ominous trees, and two praying angel statues on each side of the sidewalk entrance were enough to make one feel creeped out. It had an old wooden porch with a swing that swayed when the wind was blowing just right. It was like something out of a classic horror movie; the first look at Whispers Estate was unsettling.

I parked my car along the sidewalk in front of the house. India and I got out, grabbed some of our gear from the trunk, and made our way past the two angel statues and onto the wooden porch where we rang the doorbell. I stood impatiently as I anticipated my first steps into the house.

Please speak with me tonight spirits. I would love to get to know your story. I need this, I said, thinking to myself. I stared at the front door that had no windows. I could not see inside and the anticipation was killing me. The porch started to vibrate. It was someone's footsteps from the other side of the door, coming to see what strange person could be here this time. The knob started to turn, the door swung open and a woman with short blonde hair greeted us; it was Sondra. She smiled and told us to come in.

As the two of us made our way through the door, Sondra told us that Rich was running late and that he should arrive at the house at any moment. I nodded my head as my way of answering her. My eyes wandered tirelessly as I looked at everything that I could humanly absorb around me. I was like a dog refusing to look away from its treat.

I noticed a set of stairs to my right, a room called the parlor to my left, and a wooden floor hallway that lead straight to what appeared to be a dining room. The house had a particular smell about it. It was not a bad smell. It was something between a normal house smell and the kind I familiarize with from visiting other haunted locations.

We got to the dining area where a massive wooden table sat in the middle of the room. Sondra told us we could set our gear down on the table. I looked over at India. She took the gear she was carrying and set it down and I did the same. Sondra walked around the table to face India and me.

My eyes once again started to roam my surroundings. Around the dining area were many other things to gaze an eye upon. A fireplace was on the left side of the room with an Ouija board that sat on the mantelshelf right above it. In fact, Ouija boards were everywhere around the home. This is a common method paranormal investigators have been keen on using when attempting communication here.

• ≒≡⧼◆❍◉◖◍◗≡⧽ ┼ •

As I observed the things around me, there were three doorways that left the dining area. There was a doorway on the left side of the fireplace that lead into a room with two long brown couches and a glass display case that held antique items. Another door was in that room that lead to an area that appeared to be doctor themed area with a bed. An old medical coat hung on a hanger with the last name Gibbons patched on it.

On the other side of the big wooden table in the dining area, past the fireplace, and straight ahead was a doorway that led into the kitchen. This is where the basement entrance was, a set of stairs on the left side that lead upstairs, and a walk-in closet converted room called The Harry Potter closet. This is a place Sondra stays in while paranormal investigators explore the house in case they need anything.

The third doorway was on the left side of the brown couch room doorway. It was almost directly behind me from where I was standing in the dining area; this led into The Parlor room.

Whenever Sondra spoke, I had this uncontrollable urge to focus my vision over her shoulder, into the kitchen, and towards the staircase to the second floor. As our conversations carried on, I for some reason felt like I was being watched. It almost made me uncomfortable. My stomach started to turn. Nothing was at the staircase at any given moment that I looked, or at least nothing that I could see.

This house felt different than any other place I had gone to up to this point in my paranormal journey. It created an invisible surge that drew out the anxiety within my brain. I caught myself a few times attempting to convince my consciousness that this was nothing more than something that I was simply imagining.

CHAPTER FOUR
THERE IS DEATH IN THIS HOUSE

It wasn't long after spending time talking to Sondra when I heard the front door open and shut from behind me. My back was facing the wooden hallway when I turned and looked at who it was. A man smiled, putting his hand up in greeting as he walked in our direction and introduced himself.

"Hey, I'm Rich," he said, reaching his hand out to shake mine. I looked down at his hand and extended mine.

It was the owner of Whispers Estate who walked through the door. As we shook hands, he started apologizing for his tardiness. I reassured him that everything was okay and that we appreciated him allowing us to investigate. Rich was wearing a black leather jacket, a black polo shirt with black jeans. He had

47

ridden his motorcycle to the house, which is most likely why he was late due to traffic he encountered from his hour drive from his work; Rich is a professor at a school.

He told us that he was not able to stay long as he had to grade papers for the morning and asked if he could do his interview first. The sun was quickly going down and without hesitation, we agreed. I proceeded to grab from our gearbox what I needed for this segment of our show. I gave Rich a wireless microphone to put on for his audio, grabbed the main camera I was going to use, made sure the settings were correct, and then handed India the one that she was going to use.

Rich wanted to start his interview on the second floor in a room they call, 'Jessie's Room'. This was the first time that India and I were going to go upstairs and I had no idea what to expect to be told. Rich led the way with India following behind him and me behind her. We walked to the staircase next to the front door and began to ascend the wooden steps. Rich and India took their first steps onto the second floor, I was almost to the

top when I noticed a painting that was no longer obscured from my view. It was a long skinny painting of what appeared to be a body. It was unsettling to gaze upon because this was the only picture like this around the house. So much so that I had to ask what this was all about.

"What is that painting of?" I asked Rich.

"Oh, that is something that was painted when the previous owners had the house. They believe that there are bodies somewhere buried in the backyard. The painting is suppose to be a representation of that."

This was something I was completely unaware of. I held my tongue to ask why because I wanted to have that story told on camera. The hallway on the second floor came into view. It had white-painted walls that warped to the right in a quarter circle shape. It too had wooden floors with five doorways. Two on the left, two on the right, and one at the end of the hallway. The first door on the left was 'Jessie's room', where Rich was taking us. The first door on the right was a small room with some creepy dolls and stairs that led to the third floor of the house.

As we stepped into 'Jessie's room', we hadn't begun recording on our cameras just yet when Rich started to give us some information on some of the paranormal experiences people have had while investigating the house. I was still making sure our lighting was good.

I don't mind people telling me about paranormal experiences before we start the interview, but I like to hear it for the first time while on camera. I find that it's common for stories to lose some detail when asked to be retold. However, he made a bold claim of audio he said to be in possession of from a team who investigated a closet on the second floor in an area known as The Servant's Quarters; the room at the end of the hallway.

Rich told us that a man had a heart attack, fell over, and died in the closet area. Paranormal investigators were doing an EVP (electronic voice phenomenon) session in hopes of communicating with this man. The closet is big enough for a few people to comfortably sit inside and this is how they were doing it with the door shut. Rich pulled out his cellphone and started to play the audio recording they sent to him.

I could hear multiple people asking questions, and attempting contact. A few moments into the recording, a child greets himself, and then everyone reacts and starts to freak out. I immediately noticed it as well. It sounded like a child was with them. Rich informed us that there were no children present during that investigation. I found this so interesting that I too wanted to have this happen. If this was a genuine piece captured inside the Whispers Estate, it was extremely compelling and it definitely freaked me out.

Jessie's room has a bed with a canopy, a small skinny couch, a mustard-colored plush chair, and a walk-in closet; known to Whispers Estate as Gary's closet. The walls had a light purple color with pictures that hung all around. It looked like this room was still being occupied; but not by the living.

I finished placing our lighting where it needed to be, I hit the record button on my camera to capture anything more that

Rich might say. He then started to tell India about an experience that happens often at Whispers Estate. Rich showed her a picture on his cellphone of a woman's neck. She had multiple red markings. This is when he said this woman in the picture was scratched eleven times in one night in this particular room. Because of these attacks, the group packed up their things and ended their investigation. I needed to know why this was happening.

"I hope you guys have some activity," said Rich, "Once again, I think I told you on the phone we can't guarantee you'll experience anything.....but."

"Oh yeah. I know," I replied. Although we were on what I felt like a losing streak, I felt that this place for some reason was different. It was like I felt connected to something invisible.

I walked up to Rich to turn on his wireless microphone attached to his shirt. Rich continued, "You guys understand that. You uh....have been doing it long enough."

"Well if I hear a kid like that, I'm out," India said,

chuckling as she referred to the audio Rich played.

I laughed and agreed as I walked back over towards India's direction to grab my camera.

Rich looked over at me. "Okay. So where do you guys want me to stand? It's your show."

I pointed to an area for him to stand by the walk-in closet.

"Yeah I have like a hundred and fourteen tests to grade tonight," Rich said in laughter.

"Oh my gosh," replied India.

"Okay, don't worry, this won't take long," I said, lifting my camera up to face Rich. I started to describe how our interviews normally go and that I wanted him to feel comfortable on camera. I told him to start by saying his name, his position at Whispers Estate, and whatever ghost stories he knows or experienced.

"Okay. My name is Rich Ballard and I am the current owner of the Whispers Estate," Rich said as he then paused waiting for direction from me. I told him to tell the camera where in the house we are and to continue from there.

"Okay, my name is Richard Ballard and we are standing here in Jessie's room — on the second floor of the Whispers Estate," Richard said. "This is one of the more famous parts of the house. There seems to be lots of activity that happens for our visitors." Rich once again paused shaking his head and smiling.

"What kinds of things are people experiencing in this room?" I asked.

"Well, we've had a lot of things happen in this room. Pretty typical things that you get lots of times in some of these haunted places," Rich said. "People will get EVP recordings, doors will open, doors will shut. We do get people at times that get physically touched in this room. Whether it's their hair that gets pulled — we do get people that get scratched. We also have situations where the furniture will move with people on it."

"You said that people get touched or scratched in this room?"

"Yeah! Just recently we had a group of four women visit the house and one of the teammates, she got scratched I think she told me on the phone eleven times. This room was probably the most aggressive part of the house towards her," Rich continued. "She got scratched on her back, on her neck — and while sitting in one of these couches here....It appeared that something had smacked her. After about that many contacts with her, the group ended their investigation prematurely."

"Do people get scratched here a lot then?" I asked, in curiosity as to what he might have thought was causing these markings.

"You know, it depends on the group. Often there are a lot of people who are touched. There is a lot of whispering in people's ears. One of the reasons the house got its name is because of a lot of the interaction with whatever is in the house — it is a very soft voice, almost like a whisper. But we do get lots of visitors who get scratched. It is usually females; we don't have any idea as to why that's the case. There are lots of people with theories but once again, those are just theories. It's pretty hard to prove when it comes to something like that."

"Now that closet door—," I said pointing behind Rich. "–You showed us something. What significance does that closet door have in this house?" I asked.

"Well, we call that Gary's closet. Back in the 1980s, a family lived here that had a young boy named Gary. He would play — as you saw it's this huge closet...It's got toys all over. Tragically enough, the young boy passed away here in the house. And since then, visitors report that the doorknob will jiggle a little bit and of course, the closet itself will swing open. I myself have seen it happen at least a dozen times in all my visits to the house. Once again there are lots of groups who have video of it. We set up our own camera one afternoon and finally got video evidence ourselves, which we have on our website," Rich finished saying.

Already I felt this was an ideal spot for India and me to spend some time tonight investigating Jessie's room. I really wanted to capture 'Gary's closet' door opening. After all these years of doing paranormal investigating, I have never captured this kind of phenomenon happening. I was skeptical that the door was something that could be explained away but Rich demonstrated in multiple different ways that the door itself is not faulty. I watched as he jumped around in front of the closet, refusing to swing open. Rich also opened the door and shut it showing us that it will not disengage from the locking mechanism. This closet door was firmly and securely functioning as it should. So if it was not something natural that was causing this to open, then what was it and how?

"Do you have anywhere else you would like to take us in the house that you want to show us?" I asked Rich.

"Yeah, I wouldn't mind taking you to Rachael's room."

"Yeah, let's do that."

Rich proceeded to take us to the hallway and through the second door to the left. This is the area of the house for which Whispers Estate is most famous. The room had dolls everywhere and I mean everywhere you looked with different ones ranging all the way from creepy looking babies to clowns. It had one

bed with two giant beach balls that sat parallel to the other on the foot of the bed frame. There was a dresser with an attached mirror and on the counter sat a lonesome picture of a little girl. The walls were yellow with an old brick fireplace that had a wooden bookshelf in place of the firebox.

Once we were almost ready setting up the scene in Rachael's room, Rich wanted to make something clear before he continued on with his interview.

"Once again, I don't want you guys — I don't wanna contaminate your experiences too much cause I don't want you guys expecting something to happen. Often this house — has something new that happens every time people visit,"

"Yeah, we understand," I replied as Rich nodded his head, smiling. I'm not sure why he was reiterating his fear. It could be because he's seen Paranormal Encounters and had some thought that we would not capture anything. In fact, we would end up scraping the two locations we had filmed before we made

it to Whispers Estate because of some circumstances; this house, however, made this trip worth it.

"Okay. Are you ready India?"

"Yeah," she replied as she got into position making sure her camera was recording.

"Okay Rich whenever you're ready," I said.

"Okay, right now we are in Rachael's room. We call this Rachael's room because Rachael lived in the house. We think she was between the ages of nine and twelve. Tragically enough, on Christmas eve in 1912 — she had snuck downstairs to probably what we think to look under the Christmas tree — no one knows for sure." Rich continued, "However, we do know she somehow or another fell into the tree, knocking the Christmas tree on herself — of course, this is back before they were decorated with electric lights and stuff, they probably had candles on it. Tragically enough, her gown did catch on fire and she sustained second and third-degree burns all over her body. They brought her up here, her father, Dr. Gibbons, and they put her in a bed in this corner," Rich said as he pointed at where the bed was in Rachael's room, continuing, "and she did pass away unfortunately a few days later I believe on December 27th."

This explained why there was a room on the first floor decorated with medical items. This used to be the office of Dr. Gibbons, and the room before it with the two big brown couches was the waiting room. This is a tragic story. There is death in this house and it will only become more evident that Rachael was not the only one.

CHAPTER FIVE
THE HORNED ENTITY

Shortly after our interview with Rich in Rachael's room, he had to leave to grade papers for his class for the following day. I could not help but think about the story of Rachael; this is the one the home was famous for. I knew that a little girl passed away in a fire before I ever visited this house but I never knew how severe it was. When we interviewed Sondra, However, is when I realized this and just how scarred the home really is. Sondra wanted to begin her interview in The Parlor room; this is where the tragedy for Rachael started.

I told Sondra that I wanted her to talk in my direction as I was holding the main camera. I then told her that we are ready whenever she is.

She shook her head acknowledging what I said, took a deep breath, and began speaking. "I'm Sondra Burris. We are inside Whispers Estate. This is the front parlor. This house is at least from 1864. It was previously owned by Dr. White and his wife then it was sold to Dr. John Gibbons and his wife Jessie. They were known for adopting orphaned and abandoned children — they couldn't have any children of their own," Sondra said, as she walked towards the doorway that led into the dining room area.

"We do however have documentation of one daughter that was Helen Marie but the house is mostly known for Rachael. It was said that she came into this room to sneak a peek at some Christmas gifts. Over here in the pocket door...." Sondra began to pull a sliding door from a crack in the entryway. "You will see burnt evidence on the door here," Sondra said, pointing at the areas where it has been clearly burned.

Charred wood was all over the door. The cracked scars stuck out like crocodile scutes. It was evident that a severe fire took place and was burning these areas that were damaged for a while. Sondra told India and I that Rachael was presumably pinned in the doorway from the Christmas tree. She even showed us evidence that the fire stretched across the room into the main doorway from the wooden floor hallway. This event was forever burned into the house as a constant reminder of that tragic night.

Sondra took us back upstairs to Rachael's room to give us a shocking twist into how Rachael's death actually happened and it was not from the burns she sustained from the accident. She told India and I that after the fire, her father Dr. John Gibbons took Rachael back to her bedroom to give her treatment. Three days later, in fear of what the community might think, he administered a lethal dose of morphine to her and she passed away in her room on December 27th, 1912. Sondra said that Whispers Estate wants to believe it was a mercy killing but said that legend and lore Dr. Gibbons viewed her as 'damaged goods' and was afraid that she might ruin his reputation.

— ⋮═◦❯◉❮◦═⋮ —

The part that I find difficult with this story of Rachael is the fact that I can not find any death records or anything that ties her to be a real person. I even went as far as to search the county records and found nothing. The Gibbons did, however, have a daughter named Helen Marie Gibbons Dobel who passed away in 1994. She would have been five months old around the time that Rachael would have died.

Sondra then took us into 'Jessie's room' once again to give us more information on how Gary passed away; the little boy who is said to open the closet.

Sondra walked over to the door and began talking in the direction of my camera.

"In the late 1970s', there was a little boy that lived here, his name was Gary. So he use to play hide-n-seek and things like that. So his family said, if he ever went missing they always knew where to find him; that of course was in the linen closet."

Sondra went on to reiterate what Rich told us about the paranormal claims but told us the tragic story of how Gary died.

He too met his fate within the walls of Whispers Estate. He had somehow fallen to the bottom of the wooden steps by the front door. That is one of the stories told to Whispers Estate about how he died. The other version was that Gary was a special needs child and a medical equipment piece in his neck malfunctioned, causing his death.

We followed Sondra to the hallway to stop in front of the second door on the right. This area sure enough was a bathroom. It was not a big room, but rather a skinny rectangle shape area with an old fashion claw-foot bathtub; with a toilet and sink.

Whispers Estate was once a boarding house where income-driven families could rent out rooms. This was well before anyone reported the home to be haunted.

"This bathroom here, we had a renter here who rented out the second floor at the time. He was getting out of the bathtub..... he slipped and broke his neck. Laid here for about three days. His name was Henderson or Hindelson. But when he slipped and fell, nobody found him cause it was in the middle of Summer before someone found him. We have a lot of people who get in there and have trouble breathing," Sondra said, pointing at the bathtub. "We have EVPS in there of 'Help me' with apparitions going from one wall to the other....As well as coming out."

"And that's the actual bathtub?" India asked.

Sondra reached her hand to grab the doorknob of The Servant's Quarters.

"Yes. That bathtub is original to the house,"

We followed her into the room. Each step I took I could hear the wooden floors creak below my feet. It reminded me of the same kind of sound from a scene in a horror movie.

Sondra walked over to the farthest wall to turn on a light fixture that hung above the stairs in the middle of the room; these went to the first floor and led into the kitchen. The Servants Quarters had a wood church pew, a round table with two chairs with an Ouija board in the middle of it, and a closet that had two swing-open doors. The walls were painted in two separate dividing colors. The left side of the room was white. This had the closet and the round table with the Ouija board; the yellow side had the church pew, and a plush chair.

After Sondra flipped the light switch on, she turned around to face us and once again looked in the direction of my camera, describing where we were.

"This is what we call 'The Servants Quarters'," she began saying. "We don't have any documentation that Dr. John had any servants. However, I was telling you about Gary the nine year old boy — they rented this floor, his dad when they moved out came back to get a hammer and a ladder — "

Sondra walked over to the closet with the two swing-open doors. She started to unlock it and open it while continuing.

"When he opened these closet doors to get that hammer and ladder, Gary's dad had a fatal heart attack."

The closet had a table with two chairs that sat next to each other. This is the same closet that Rich told us where a paranormal investigation team was inside when they captured a child talking to them during their conversation amongst themselves while in the dark with the audio captured on their voice recorders.

"We cleaned this out," Sondra continued, "and started letting people investigate in here. It started off with small scratches and stuff. That wasn't really a big deal because thats something that's common here. But it started escalating to where a 19 year old was chocked so violently she had to be driven home."

Now, I get asked all the time "Connor, aren't you scared? Aren't you afraid something will attack you? The simple answer is no, the complicated answer is why I'm not. I think it just comes down to my personal belief. And that is that I don't believe in it. I have never had it happen to me and that isn't to say that it is not a thing that happens. It just has never happened to me and if it does I would want to experience it. It sounds crazy but it fascinates me. I want to understand if this is some invisible force that has the grip of a human hand or is this just the feeling that gives the impersonation like one is being choked.

Sondra started to close the closet doors and began discussing something that I had no idea was a thing at this house.

"We also had people investigate in here and these doors fly open and something pounds on these doors like something wants out. We've seen horned entities in here. We were doing a table tipping session in the nursery," she said, pointing towards the hallway we had just come from. This is the room across from where John and Jessie's bedroom was.

Sondra pointed in my direction.

"There was something standing at the end of this banister. It was like it was looking down the hallway."

Sondra took a deep anxious breath and slowly let it out. I could tell this was an experience that shook her up and that was hard for her to look back on.

She crossed her wrists with her arms extended down to her waist. "It was standing like this. It had a human figure but it had a goat face with horns that went up and around," she said, demonstrating a swirly motion next to her ears. "I was with two

77

other people when I seen this. Now, I won't repeat what I said but I asked, what is that? And when they looked up, they also seen this. We were closest to Rachael's room and we ducked into her room. We stayed for a good amount of time before we looked out and looked down to see if this was gone — It was," Sondra continued, "It didn't seem threatening by any means, of course, it was scary. That is the only time that I have ever seen anything in here."

Sondra walked towards and down the wooden stairs that led into the kitchen area. We quietly followed behind her. She took us to the back part of the kitchen where a small bathroom was, She flipped the light on, moved to the left to stand in another doorway with two doors, and began to describe why we stopped in this particular area.

"This bathroom here. We were told by a historian that this was probably used as the morgue. That's because Dr. John didn't have to store the bodies that long."

Sondra turned to point at the door directly behind her. On

the other side was the office room of Dr. Gibbons.

"So this use to be the other door to the surgery room. So he could have just brought them over here and store them."

Sondra then turned to her left, grabbed a sliding lock to unlock, and opened the other door. Without saying anything, she started walking down into the basement. As we approached the cement floor at the bottom steps, I told India that I had around a minute left on my camera's battery before it died. Sondra assured us that our time in the basement would take less than a minute.

"This is the basement area. A lot of things happen down here."

Sondra walked over to a long picnic table that had metal chairs that surrounded it.

"It like to move this table," she continued. "We're not sure what it is. It likes to pull your hair. Throw things off people's heads."

Sondra turned her body and pointed at the corner behind the picnic table. "Something back in that area acts like a portal.

A lot of things down here like to tell you to get out while your down here."

Sondra paused for a moment and then told us that this would be the end of the tour. I stopped recording on my camera and within seconds of doing this, my camera died. I was relieved that I was able to have just enough time to capture everything she was talking about. If it had died while I was recording her, there is a chance that the footage would have been lost due to not properly stopping the camera.

It is because of these stories from Sondra that I had no idea of the amount of history behind Whispers Estate. I was eagerly excited for our overnight paranormal investigation. The sun was dropping in the sky and I had something that I needed to take care of before the lights go out.

CHAPTER SIX
THE HOME IS ALIVE

Whispers Estate was ranked the fourth most haunted place in The United States by a show called, Most Terrifying Places in America. I can see why, as this house will draw a person in like an addict that seeks its dose. A trance that imprisons one's eyes while wandering the hallways, admiring what comes into view.

During the interviews, I could sense that something was shifting and that something of invisible nature was watching me from around every corner. At some points, I had to look twice thinking that I had captured something from the corner of my eye.

There are places that I have traveled to that were said to be highly active with paranormal phenomena. I spent countless hours roaming throughout the night and witnessed nothing at the majority of these locations. This house, however, I could feel was haunted. I felt this sensation throughout my entire body. It is like the mental tingling of the mind. In a way, it is the same feeling one might have when something good or bad is about to happen in the pit of the stomach. This is the intuition from within speaking softly in the ear. A somewhat cloudy tunnel vision while in the moment. Something important was going to take place this night; I felt this.

When we concluded our interview with Sondra and I proceeded to the dining area where the massive wooden table sat. I picked up my gear bag. Inside had memory cards and a charged battery for my camera. I took out the old one and replaced it with a new one along with an empty memory card. I did this because I wanted to separate the interviews from the footage we shot around the house. I have always been superstitious and overlay protective while filming. There are only two of us in this show with each of us having our own camera; if a memory card were to get lost, so would the episode. So, over the years I have developed the habit of switching memory cards each time that I am done filming and taking a break.

The sun was setting and it was quickly getting dark. I went outside to the backyard of Whispers Estate to set up a time-lapse on my phone of the sunset. This was also a perfect time for me to film the remainder of the exterior shots I needed. The house started to get eerily creepy as the evening got darker. The cloudless sky was overcast gray and it swallowed the white siding of the house in its entirety.

I stood on the grassy lawn looking at my surroundings. The backyard had an old small white shed where trees stood along with the surrounding property, causing very little light. This was a much darker surrounding; I felt like I was starring in some sort of horror movie. The stories that were told during the interview with Sondra and Rich were haunting. A classic ghost story only, I was walking through the pages. I could not get this Rachael tragedy out of my mind. I also couldn't help but wonder if the painting at the top of the wooden stairway to the second floor had any merit of being true. Could there be any bodies buried beneath the soil? There is so much legend and lore behind Whispers Estate that I wouldn't be surprised if there was.

While writing this book I interviewed Sondra over a video call to ask for her opinion on whether or not she felt this was possible. The answer remains open. It is believed that if this were to be true, Rachael, her brother, and another child would be those who are one with the grounds of Whispers Estate. A sort of haunting idea as their bodies would be long gone and part of the soil upon which the house rests. Making Rachael and the children she was laid to rest with, part of this ghostly home that nestles in a quiet town in southern Indiana.

The more time I spent outside filming, the more I started to feel that this ghost story was a perfect addition to our paranormal encounters journey. It felt unique from the start and I could feel that this investigation was not going to be like any of the other ones that I had done in the past. There is a part of me that wanted us to be the ones who discovered and somehow proved that Rachael was more than a myth.

I spent roughly an hour into the peak part of the sunset before feeling I had everything that I needed. I gathered my things and made my way back inside the house to regroup with India. She was going to help me film the areas we were taken to during our interviews. I had her hold the lighting while I set up the creepy shots and the items of significance that went with the ghost stories. We eventually went into the nursery across from Rachael's room and went up the stairs that led to the third floor.

This was the area where I had seen a lot of people film themselves using the Ouija board when I first found out about Whispers Estate. The third floor I was told was not open at the time when Dr. Gibbons occupied the house with his family.

There weren't many paranormal experiences told to us during the interviews that gave us any indication for this floor of the house to be our focus. However, India and I did have some odd things happen to us while we were filming clips for our video. This was when unexplainable things began to happen.

The stairway walls to the third floor of the house are unfinished. White striped paint runs randomly and vertically along the pale yellow painting going upstairs. This floor is still under renovation and if it was my guess, this was once a lonely attic with nothing but its wooden floors.

• ::═◄•◗◉◖•►═:: •

At the top of the stairs, rested a four brick long support wall that split the three rooms and a walk-in closet apart. The first room we went into was the first entrance at the top of the stairs on the right. This is called The Seance Room and where I had seen the majority of YouTube videos about Whispers Estate take place. Paranormal investigators use this room to communicate to the spirits of the house with a talking board or voice recorders.

I personally do not believe in these boards from my experience of using them with nothing happening to myself. This isn't to say they don't work, I am just the type of person

88

who has a healthy skepticism about anything said to be used to communicate with ghosts; I have to experience something to accept the idea of a technique.

We had to duck our heads while walking through the doorway and step down into a triangle-shaped section that had four metal chairs surrounding a wooden round table with a rhombus-shaped mirror on the wall behind it. This was an eerie sight to see; the room was enclosed except for a section on the step-down part of this room. Parts of the wall were still in the process of being built as its wooden studs bore nakedness where one could see into a room on the other side.

This room was odd. Behind the four studs were several old wooden chairs and a bed. There wasn't a mattress to be seen only a note asking to not sit on it.

The walk-in closet had a part that made it unique. This was not any ordinary closet, this part of the third floor is called The Oculus Room. It gets its name for the entire circumference inside being covered in mirrors. This gives the illusion of some

sort of dimension with an endless reflection no matter what angle one looks at. It's very disorienting but a clever idea. It was told to us off-camera by Rich that he and others had seen figures in these mirrors. Unfortunately, we could not use this room at the time of our visit because it was still in the process of being finished and some mirrors still needed to be glued in place. I did not see any point in filming the walk-in-closet.

We then went into the final room called the 'Red Room'. The name speaks for itself. The walls, couch, bed sheets, pillows; everything is red. I was filming a shot of the bed while India held our lighting. It was mere seconds into this clip when four distinct creaking sounds echoed from the wooden stairway we had just come up. It resembled the sound of small footsteps quickly tapping away from us.

"Is that a joke?" India cried out.

The two of us quickly looked in that direction. At the moment I thought it was Sondra coming up to see what we were doing or even perhaps wanted to watch us film.

"He-Hello?" I yelled out in a stutter.

We stood quietly and stared in silence, waiting to see who was responsible for this disruption. I could only hear a car's engine as it drove by from the outside. Nothing seemed to make an appearance. A skin-crawling feeling overtook me.

"Are you filming?"

"Yeah," I responded, as I moved my camera and followed behind her walking towards the sound to investigate its cause.

"Hello?" India cried out, as she stepped to the doorway to the hall and paused in her tracks.

We stood quietly, listening for any more of these weird sounds. It was distinct. I knew they were footsteps.

"Where was that coming from? Back there or?"

"From the stairs," I interrupted.

India then started walking towards the stairs and peeked around the corner to the right to look down. I quickly rushed past her to look as well. Nothing. Not a soul was in sight, not even Sondra.

"What the Hell was that?" I verbally questioned. I then walked back towards and into The Red Room. India followed me and said that it sounded like it was someone moving. I quickly finished the shot I was trying to do moments ago and then told India that I was done being on the third floor. I felt creeped out.

Looking back on the events that occurred, it was like something was watching what we were doing, following us, and then quickly running away. This could explain how India thought she saw legs moving and the sound of small footsteps fleeing.

Although we had these things happen, we weren't told that many stories of paranormal experiences that gave any idea that this area of the house would be a focus in the dark. I wanted to mainly attempt communication with Rachael or the man who fell and broke his neck on the second-floor bathroom.

This was all the footage that I needed for our episode. By this time it was dark outside and we were ready to start our investigation of the Whispers Estate.

CHAPTER SEVEN
OUR ADVENTURE BEGINS IN THE DARK

It was a little past eight that night when India and I left Whispers Estate for almost an hour. We finished filming the interviews and shots of the house and it was now time for our adventure in the dark. The cameras were left charging, and we went looking to do so ourselves.

Doing a paranormal exploration in the dark just doesn't feel completely satisfying without having a nice meal beforehand. It takes a lot of energy out of a person. It's not just because one stays up all hours of the night with endless sleep like some sort of vampire. It's because it consists of foreign exploration of hallways and rooms of a place I've never been — like a sailor lost at sea. It's hours of asking questions out loud to myself like

97

I'm interrogating the air that flows in front of me. It is definitely like being in a real-life horror movie. The adrenaline rushes throughout my body as I anticipate the unknown that could lurk around every corner.

Every hour that I'm not in the location I paid to film at is time lost in my eyes. I rarely feel satisfied with the limited amount of time allocation we're allowed to have at the majority of locations I have been to. Time, however, is irrelevant when it comes to the paranormal. I feel that this concept has no existence within the realm of the supernatural.

It's weird to admit, but I feel that when I'm deep in the dark exploring paranormal activity, I have one foot in their world and one in our own — it's like being in two places at once. It's experiencing what was and what still is all at the same time. It's communicating with something of a time that was once what someone knew of and at the same time communicating with what hadn't changed because that essence stopped at that very moment. The best that I can describe this experience is like feeling foggy yet having a mesmerizing feeling. It can be addicting. I crave the unbelievable. It makes me feel attached to places; I hate leaving them. It takes days or even weeks for me to fully feel gone from them.

It was only a short amount of time that we were away from Whispers Estate getting dinner and it was enough of a taste for that craving to kick in. The stuff we experienced on the third floor just before we left was all it took to grab my attention. I began to feel this tingling sensation that started from the back of my head and crawl its way slowly down my neck. It was almost too slow that it was like an uncomfortable itch I couldn't scratch. Maybe it was just my social anxiety kicking in because I was in a public place. It could also have been that I hate waiting for the check while eating at restaurants. My mind was already back at Whispers Estate but my physical body wasn't. Believe me, I ate less than I should have at dinner because of this.

I remember the way back to the house, the turn down the streetlight illuminated road where Whispers Estate sat felt ominous. The neighborhood was quiet. Not a sound from the world was heard; it was like watching a silent movie. It was the calm before the storm; a storm I had no idea was coming.

The house was hidden from view as we got closer because the trees out front cloaked it in darkness. It was when we parked our car along the sidewalk out front where it only then stuck out. My stomach curled as I gazed at its structure. The moonlight illumination was perfect. It was just enough to see the shadows from the trees above the angel statues that guarded what lay behind them. This is my favorite part when starting my exploration in seeking the paranormal — turning off the lights. There is nothing that compares to what it feels like to be submerged in total darkness. It's funny how we take away our vision as this is the most common practice for communicating with the paranormal at night. People often ask why it's always done at night? This is because the world is much quieter. Less people are walking the sidewalks, and a few, if any, cars drive by. Shadows from the outside world also no longer cast through the windows at night, creating false paranormal evidence down the hallways. Although, Whispers Estate has covered all their windows, blocking out the light from the outside world from bleeding in. This makes you feel like you're stepping inside an alternate world. While everyone is sleeping, we attempt communication with the forever sleeping. When we take away our vision, our other senses are heightened and it sort of is like I'm navigating through a *thick black fog*.

It was only the three of us in the house. It was India, myself, and Sondra. She stayed in the kitchen in a tiny closet turned room she called, *The Harry Potter Closet*. Sondra was going to rest her eyes and be in the house if we needed her for anything.

As this house does have three floors, we decided to start our paranormal investigation on the first floor in the Parlor room and work our way up. India had the idea of using a device that's popular on our show called the Portal in hopes of possibly communicating with the little girl, Rachael. This room is where

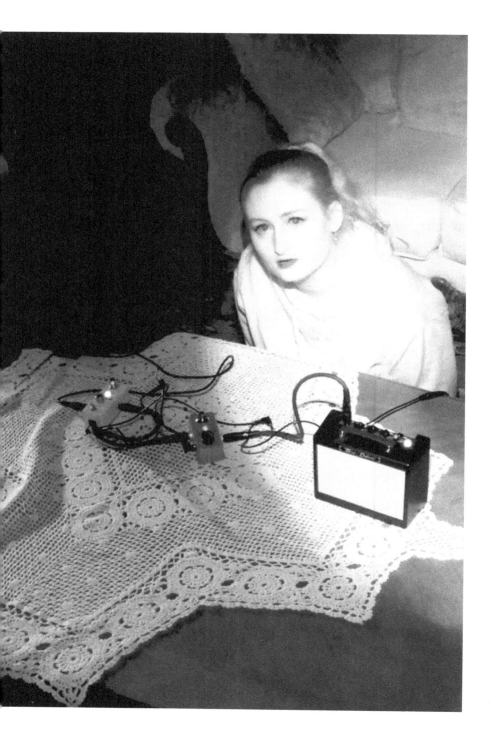

she suffered the burns from the Christmas tree lighting on fire and could potentially be one of her last memories in her living life. I just needed something to happen that would indicate that this little girl was indeed not just myth and lore.

The Portal is a modified device that enhances the input of a spiritbox, a modified radio. The purpose is to scan radio stations continuously at milliseconds of speed. When words come through the speakers from asking questions, it then goes through a reverb and noise gate guitar pedal. The reverb helps the voices last longer and the noise gate reduces the white noise from the radio stations sweeping through dead air. In theory, this is supposed to be more effective in communicating with the unknown rather than the traditional use of a spiritbox. In the years of paranormal explorations at other locations where I have used this Portal, I have been blown away by the responses received at times I could not disprove the results.

We had planned to set up our Portal session using two different camera angles in the Parlor. I stationed one of them in the corner where the wide entrance into the Parlor, closest to the stairs was. I wanted this to be our static shot that records the entire room. I placed the tripod the camera sat on next to an outlet. I had no idea how long this session was going to last because sometimes we spend almost an hour trying to get a response to come through the Portal. I had the idea of directly plugging the camera charging cord into the outlet to have continuous power to prevent the battery from dying in the middle of the session. The last thing I needed was to only have one camera recording. I only had to worry about the memory card space, which I had checked and it was plenty of space left to last for the next couple of hours.

The other camera was the main one we used during the interviews and I was going to handheld this while standing across from India near the doorway to the dining room. She wanted to set up the Portal on the coffee table and sit on the floor. India was going to be the one controlling the settings on the Portal: she just has this naturalness in finding the right setting for obtaining communication. Sometimes I feel India connects with the spirits easier than I do because I have tried to get the Portal to work while doing solo sessions, but just cannot. I never seem to have the special touch that she has and I'll always envy that. I also placed a REM pod on a chair directly behind me. This device creates a field around itself and if it is broken, the lights on the REM pod will go off. In theory, it is said that spirits can use this as an indication of their presence.

I asked India if she was ready and she told me that she was. I flipped the light switch off on the wall; we were now in total darkness, and so begins our adventure in the dark.

I walked closer to the coffee table, stopped, and faced the camera toward India.

"Ready?" asked India.

"Mmhm," I replied.

"Okay. So, right now we are in the Parlor," India began. "Where the little girl, Rachael had a Christmas tree fall on her. It caused her to be severely burned uh —," India was interrupted

105

by a temperature change beeping from the REM pod. This happened four times with a three-second pause between each beep. This is not the same light that goes off when a spirit is believed to of broken the field it puts around itself, but a single red light in the middle of the device that flashes. This tells us that the temperature has rapidly changed near the REM pod. An old traditional belief is that spirits create cold spots.

The REM pod was silent for a moment before another beep flashed its red light. "I think it's the battery dying. Because it's doing it again," India suggested.

I stood quiet. The beeping ceased. India picked up where she left off before she was interrupted.

"So um, Rachael died a few days after she was burned. We're going to do a Portal session in this room to see if we can communicate with Rachael or anybody else who may be here." India turned the Portal device on. A subtle white noise bled through the speaker.

"Rachael, are you in here with us?" I cried out.

India started to turn the knobs on the Portal, attempting to reduce the white noise and obtain a setting that produced clear tones. I started to hear the REM pod scream behind me. The temperature started changing again. Only this time, the beeping was like it was being held down. The temperature was falling very fast according to the device. It lasted for six seconds and then once again ceased.

India asked me to hit a button on the REM pod that resets the room temperature indication to level it out with what the current one is. Maybe the battery was dying or something faulty was going on with the REM pod. We weren't taking this as something paranormal at the time but looking back at these events that soon follow after this may point otherwise.

"So, if there is anybody here with us tonight, my name is India and this is Connor. We just want to communicate with you," India began. "If you are here, could you come through and talk with us?"

The Portal's rhythmic static echoed.

Scur cur scur

The vocal tone responses continued to be silent.

"Can you tell us your name?" I asked.

Scur cur scur

"How many of you are living here?" India asked.

Scur cur scur

"How many children are in this house?" I asked.

Scur cur scur

Inaudible, vocal tones started to come through the Portal. India started turning more knobs trying to make those more clear when she accidentally turned a wrong knob that blew out a very loud reverberated static noise. It was so loud that I had to take a few steps back. India quickly turned the Portal off and then back on to keep that noise from echoing any further.

Scur cur scur

It was now back to sounding more normal.

"Rachael. Are you here?" India cried out.

Some voices were coming through. Once again inaudible.

"Dr. John, is that you?"

Scur cur scur

I moved a little to my right to get a better shot of the Portal and India. The static continued to chime as we remained quiet, listening for something to come through the speakers.

"Jessie? India cried out once more.

The Portal rumbled.

We waited for a moment in silence, just listening for something when a raspy male's voice came through.

"*Hey*"

India looked up at me in relief that we had captured our first something.

"Hi," she answered, back to this unknown voice.

"It just said hey?" I asked, confirming what I too thought was said.

"Yeah," India answered with a nod, then directed her attention back to the Portal.

"How are you doing?" she asked.

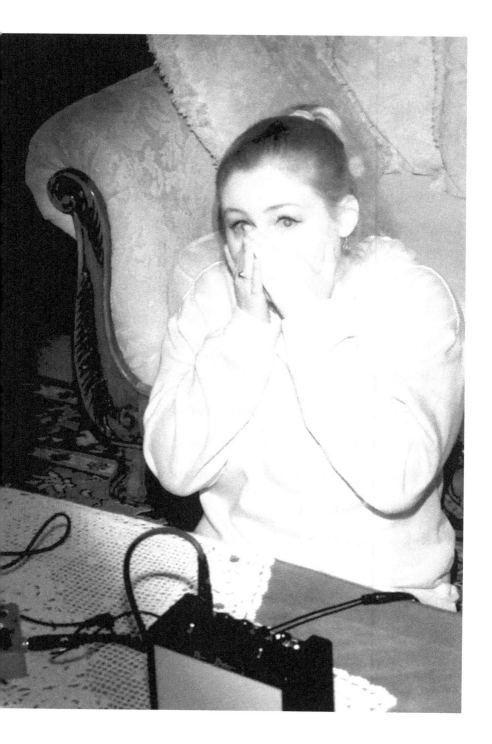

Static continued to come through the speakers. A loud chime-like noise echoed and India was quick to grab one of the knobs on the Portal, taking a few seconds to adjust the reverb.

"What room are you in?" India asked.

Chur chur chur chur chur chur

"RACHAEL," yelled out a middle-aged woman's voice through the Portal.

India's eyes got huge. She threw her hands up to cover her mouth as her jaw had dropped simultaneously when her eyes became huge; it was adrenaline and realization all at once.

I *gasped.*

"Are you kidding me?" India exclaimed.

"It just said Rachael," I stated in confidence.

India and I could not believe how clear this response was. The fact that the little girl's voice came through the Portal is undeniably amazing. The fact that I must get across is that there is absolutely no way for this to of happened. It's a radio. Nothing that we say or ask can be manipulated and spoken back through

the speakers. There is no input or recording device. This has to be something paranormal.

If it is not, then it is one hell of a coincidence for the name Rachael to be spoken. I was extremely thrilled. This was the first location on this road trip that provided the feeling that maybe something is here. Maybe there is something to the ghost story after all and we were just scratching the surface.

We were only nine minutes into the Portal session and we had already without a doubt captured something phenomenal. We were also in the room where this fire occurred and I wanted to know more about what happened this night. This was also not a little girl's voice. So who's was it? Was it Jessie? Was it an echo of the moment she saw Rachael trapped in the Christmas tree?

India and I gathered ourselves and quickly got back to our Portal session. She apologized out loud to this voice for freaking out and that it just took her by surprise when she heard the name, Rachael. I think anyone who was with us when this came through the Portal would have acted the same.

"Rachael, are you here?" asked India.

The REM began indicating that the temperature was changing. The beeping was almost like morse code.

I yelled out.

"Are you Rachael that's in here with us?"

"Are you sitting in the chair?" asked India.

A man and woman could be heard talking but we weren't sure what was being said. India was trying to keep the communication going as I continued recording her interaction with the Portal.

"Rachael, my name is India. Can you see me?"

The Portal rumbled, without vocal tone.

We continued to ask questions, but nothing was as clear as the woman yelling out Rachael was coming through.

"I can not believe it just said that. That was so clear," India stated.

I agreed. "Rachael, were you coming down the stairs to see what Christmas presents you were having?"

Scur cur scur

"Rachael, I want to help you. Is there anything that I can do for you?" asked India.

The Portal started giving off random high and low pitch tones through the speakers. Nothing seemed to be working no matter what question was being asked. India continued to ask questions. She felt that we were on to something and I as well did not want to lose this communication.

"Am I speaking to Rachael or am I speaking with someone else?"

Just then, despite the loudness of the Portal, I thought I heard *something* move from in the dining room. I swung my night vision camera around and looked at the LCD screen to see if there was someone there. But there wasn't. Maybe it was just my mind playing tricks on me or maybe it was just paranoia settling in. Being in total darkness can do that to a person because the other senses become more heightened.

I couldn't say this was nothing and I had to call it out.

115

"I just heard a noise, India!"

"Where?"

"I don't know where, I heard it in here," I said, pointing into the dining room. I stopped at the doorway and slowly turned my camera around to face India. The temperature change immediately started beeping again on the REM pod. Maybe the device picked up a slight breeze from when I turned back around to face India and this was just a false positive.

"Is this your house?" India asked the Portal.

The REM pod was still beeping

Beeep beep beeeep

An older man's voice came through the speakers.

"Answers," he replied.

"Answers." India said, pointing at the Portal. "It said answers."

I questioned out loud.

"Answers?"

The REM pod abruptly stopped beeping.

"Are you sitting in the chair? Can you sit in the chair for me?" India asked.

I began speaking out to Rachael and informed her that we brought that device for her as a Christmas gift. I then instructed her on how to get the lights to shine.

The Portal was not giving off any voices. It was just random tones for a few moments. I started to lose some patience waiting for something as clear and definitive as the woman's voice we captured just a few moments ago.

I took my time and walked slowly away from the dining room doorway. "Rachael, do you want to play?"

Chur chur chur chur chur chur

I was beginning to think whoever it was that spoke to us either moved on or is choosing to remain quiet. Watching and observing us somewhere nearby.

"Are you still with us?" I yelled out. "My name is Connor and this is India. We just want to talk with you tonight and get to know your story."

117

I started to have a subtle feeling of sorrow.

"We just want to help you."

In my own belief, I don't feel that I could have helped this spirit but by documenting more things on camera that I couldn't explain, I may attract more people that would visit after us who may get more details about what happened that Christmas Eve night. I also feel that there could be a message the spirit wants to say and this would be a form of helping them.

A child's voice spoke through the Portal, but it was so distorted, that I could only hear the tone that made it sound childlike.

India heard it too. "Oh, that was a kid," she stated.

"That was!"

"If you want to play with these toys we brought you, go ahead," said India.

"What do you want for Christmas?" I asked.

A man mumbled through the speakers.

"Who's the man we keep hearing?" asked India.

Chur chur chur chur chur chur

"We heard that people get scratched here. Who's doing the scratching," I asked.

"I don't feel like you want to do any harm to anybody. I think you just want to make yourself known," stated India.

Chur chur chur chur chur chur

"Where do you want us to go in the house?" I cried out asking.

Chur chur chur

"Wherever you want to," replied a man over the Portal.

"WHAT?"

"Did that just?" India paused for a moment to think. "Did that just say what I think it said?"

"Where - ev-er...."

India looked at me with a straight face and finished my sentence.

"Wherever you want."

"I did hear that!"

"Okay. Okay. We're going to go upstairs. Will you join us up there?" India asked the Portal.

The device remained silent for the next few minutes. India decided that she wanted to turn the Portal off and inform Sondra, who was in the *Harry Potter Closet*, that we captured Rachael's name being spoken. She had also wanted to ask questions to the Portal about Gary, but forgot his name and wanted to ask Sondra what his name was again.

India sat still for a moment."That was….insane."

"I can't believe it said Rachael," I replied.

"That clearly said it too. It wasn't like 'oh, maybe it said Rachael', that said Rachael. What are the odds of that happening?"

I nodded. "Yeah. It also said it in a woman's voice," I added.

"What are the odds of that? That just doesn't happen."

"Well, that's a good way to start off the night."

"Yeah."

"Alright," I said looking at India. "Let's head upstairs." Once again I thought I heard something move. I quickly turned around towards the stairs. I began panning my camera from the bottom and slowly looked up. Nothing was once again there. But that doesn't mean it couldn't see me. India started to tell me that she wanted to ask Sondra some questions before we went upstairs.

"Yeah we can do that," I said turning back around in her direction. "I just keep thinking I'm hearing something."

India got up off the floor and started walking through the dining room and into the kitchen. I followed her. I was wondering what Sondra was going to think. Has anyone else ever captured anything like this at Whispers Estate?

I just walked into the kitchen and I saw India knocking on *The Harry Potter Closet.* A few seconds later, Sondra opened the squeaky door.

"Yesss?"

"First of all," India chuckled.

121

Sondra stepped out of the closet smiling as she closed the door from behind her. I think we caught her off guard.

"Oh my God," India continued. "The Portal, clear as day said Rachael."

Sondra stared at India, speechless but with a half-smile.

India looked in my direction. "Did it not?"

"Yeah, it did," I replied.

"It said Rachael?" asked Sondra.

"It said it!" India said pointing at my camera. "We can show you it said Rachael."

I nodded. "Yeah."

"But also, my question is, what's the boys name?"

"Gary," replied Sondra.

"Gary," repeated India.

Just then, I heard a noise from behind me. My back was facing the dining room.

"Hey! Hey!" I *loudly* whispered. We got quiet and I slowly turned around to look towards where I heard the noise.

"I heard that," chimed Sondra.

"What was that?" I asked.

I paused for a moment.

"India, did you hear that?"

"No."

"I heard that," said Sondra.

"Oh my God," I smirked, chuckling off my fear. "That was weird. I just heard something. She just heard something. You didn't hear that?" I once again questioned India. Surely she had to of heard what Sondra and I both just did

India reassured her answer, "Nooo."

"It come from the front," stated Sondra.

I decided to walk and stand in the doorway of the kitchen to the dining room. From this angle, I can see through the kitchen and into the Parlor. I was filming in night vision and so I could see everything from the two rooms. My infrared light from the camera on the tripod in the Parlor also helped flood more visibility. If something was moving, I was going to capture it.

I turned my head to inform India that we still had a camera recording in there. I slowly took one step into the dining room. India started to talk to Sondra. Something moved again, but not in the dining room; it was coming from the Parlor. It sounded like the footsteps we experienced on the third floor.

This startled me.

"Hey! India! I said, in a rough whisper.

"What?"

"Something just moved in here."

We stood quiet for a moment.

I yelled with a stutter.

"Who's — Who's back there?"

I started to zoom my camera on the Parlor. I could see the other camera on the tripod that we left. I felt confident that we captured this.

"I think that other camera caught what — ever was back there." I paused for a moment. "It wasn't that I actually saw anybody. It was that I heard something move."

125

"Uh..." India continued what she was saying to Sondra.

I slowly began to take a few more footsteps closer to the Parlor. I was trying to out ninja a ghost and remain as quiet as a mouse with each step that I took. My eyes were fixated on my camera's LCD; I did not blink once. I did not want to miss anything if something was indeed still in the Parlor.

"Who's back in this hallway?" I quietly called out.

As I got closer to where this noise sounded like it was from, I could now see the entire camera on the tripod in the Parlor.

I took my first step through the doorway; nothing was there. It seemed like this noise phenomenon I kept experiencing was like some type of cat-and-mouse game. I went back into the Kitchen to talk more with Sondra and India about the three of us doing something for the next segment of the show. Sondra wanted to demonstrate the church pew in the Servant's Quarters moving with us on it. We agreed and I went to retrieve the camera in the Parlor.

127

I go to grab the camera and notice that the screen was off. This is odd, it was plugged into the AC outlet; it should still be on. I clicked a button on the camera. Nothing.

I immediately started to panic. The camera had a decent amount of life left on the battery. It should have kept it on. We were only recording for twenty minutes.

I took the camera off the tripod and unplugged it from the wall. I then pushed the power button to turn it on. It worked! I felt paranoid and decided to check the playback folder to watch the video of when I heard the noises. I thought to myself, The camera must have caught this on audio. But to my discovery, the video was missing. Nothing was showing. It was giving me an error message the second my finger was off the button.

Unable to Read Memory Card

Data Files Corrupt

Please Reformat Memory Card.

My heart sank to the pit of my stomach. I now realized what the noises I last heard in the Parlor were. It was the camera being shut off. It creates two clicking sounds. That still does not explain what the previous noises I heard before that were. The thought that it was like something was following us around the house from when we were first on the third floor. The only thing that my mind goes to when I try and comprehend what has been happening, is that this could be something childlike.

Both experiences sounded like footsteps. The third-floor experience was like something ran down the stairs. It makes sense because India thought she saw legs moving. This experience in the Parlor was like something was watching what we were doing. That is why I kept feeling like I had to look around.

There is no way the camera had any kind of malfunction as I remember hitting record, checking that the AC outlet was giving power, the memory card had plenty of space left, and the battery had some charge to sustain at least an hour. This would have meant that *something* turned the camera off manually.

Maybe the noise that I first heard when we were starting the Portal session was someone watching and when we were in the kitchen talking to Sondra, someone ran into the Parlor and shut the camera off in the middle of recording, corrupting the only other video we shot this session with. I would later confirm that the video was recorded and that the file is beyond recovering.

I frantically called out to India from the kitchen. I had to break the news to her. I would then take the memory card out of my camera, switched it to a new one, and separated it from all the others. I was not going to lose one of the clearest recordings of something unlikely to naturally occur. I started to feel that maybe, just maybe, I was really in one of America's most terrifying places; and I was knocking on its door.

CHAPTER EIGHT
WHEN IT COMES KNOCKING

I was upset about what had happened with the camera on the tripod in the Parlor and I was determined that this was not going to happen again with the next scene we wanted to film.

Before we attempted to see if the church pew could move for us, we told Sondra that we wanted to take a few minutes in Jessie's Room to try to communicate with Gary. We thought that the REM pod might be a great tool to use as it appears like a toy with all the different colored lights that flash.

We positioned it in the doorway into Jessie's Room with India and I sitting inside. The point was to see if we could capture the REM pod going off like someone was coming in or out of the room. I also wanted so badly to witness the closet door opening as Rich and Sondra had claimed. We never saw this door open. However, we did have an experience I wanted to happen. The REM pod lit up the moment I opened the closet door. My mind immediately went to the feeling that it was like someone ran out and in the hallway. A game of hiding and seek.

The most important thing that happened next with our adventure in the dark was when we decided to try this same thing again but in Rachael's room. We sat the REM pod on a chair next to the dresser with her picture. We had planned to stand in the hallway this time and ask questions but before we could make it out of the room, the REM pod started to go off.

BEEP BEEP BEEP

We walked back into the room, turned off the lights, and the night vision on our cameras.

"Do you like that toy we brought you,?" asked India

There was just something unsettling about Rachael's

room. I could feel my anxiety kicking in. The second floor for some reason was giving the feeling that it was not just India and me on it.

While we waited for the REM pod to once again light up, I placed my camera on a tripod on the right side of Rachael's bed. I had it placed in the direction of the REM pod recording most of the room.

India continued to ask questions. "Are you Rachael?"

I walked towards India and took the camera she was holding so she could turn on her voice recorder to see if she could capture any EVPs (electronic voice phenomena).

"Can you light that back up for us?" I asked. "We just walked in this room."

India placed the voice recorder on the dresser.

"If you want to.....shut me in here," India began to say.

The REM pod then beeped and flashed once as if something was signaling that this was a good idea.

India pointed at the REM pod.

135

"Yeah," she chuckled. "You want...You want me to stay in here?"

The room remained silent. It was like something was observing and just waiting for the right moments to make things happen.

"Did you get that?" India asked me. She was referring to the REM pod lighting up to asking if they wanted her to stay in the room.

I shrugged my shoulders.

"I don't know. Yeah?"

I waited for a few minutes and continued to ask questions towards the REM pod. But it continued to stay silent.

"Okay. I'm going to step out," I said, calling out to the one responsible for lighting up the REM pod.

India grabbed one of the beach balls on the end of Rachael's bed, placed headphones on, and plugged them into the spiritbox. I placed the camera I took from India on another tripod inside the room next to the bedroom door. India told me that she wanted to be shut inside, in the dark, alone, and attempt communication with Rachael. I had no problem with this as she likes to put herself in the areas that are said to be highly active and where few want to be alone.

Every place that she and I have gone to that had some relation to children, India has always had this special type of ability to connect with them. She use to be a nanny for several families years back and maybe this was why.

⸻ ⸭⸺⸢⊙⊃⊂⊙⊦⸜ ⸺⸭ ⸻

I shut the door, turned off the hallway light, walked into Jessie's Room on the other side of the wall, and waited while India did a solo session. She was alone in the room for less than ten minutes trying several things to get communication. India even balanced the beach ball on the palm of her hand, trying to get a spirit to knock it off. Nothing seemed to be speaking to her through the headphones or was using the ball as a trigger object.

India stood up from the floor and called out for me to come back into the room. I turned the hallway light back on and walked back into Rachael's room. I made sure the cameras were still recording.

"The REM pod doesn't seem to want to go off now," India stated. She sat back down on the floor against the dresser with the beach ball in front of her.

"I'm going to go down stairs, okay?" I told India.

"Mmhm."

"I have to charge the other battery."

I said this because I wanted to take a break and go down to the Parlor room. I needed to try and relax and get my mind clear. I would spend my time on social media trying to get over what had happened with our camera shutting off and the footage being corrupted. This was still weighing heavily on my mind because up to this point, that was the most substantial piece we had for our episode. Nothing prepared me for what was about to happen the rest of the night.

"I'm leaving you now."

"Byeee," India replied.

I shut the bedroom door and I made my way to the stairs. There was another door at the banister that could be closed to seal off any sound that could come from the first floor and contaminate anything India did. I shut this one too and made my way downstairs to the Parlor. She was now alone.

"Rachael, my name is India and I heard your name downstairs. If you are here, I just want to talk to you. Maybe we can play something?"

India paused.

"I brought you this," India pointed at the REM pod. "I saw you playing with it earlier or at least I saw someone playing with it. Can you let me know that was you?"

When I got to the Parlor, I sat on the couch and started to record a video on my phone. I had batteries charging at the time and I thought it would be a great idea to have just in case I needed a clip to cut for the episode. I had no idea what India was doing. At one point I could hear some subtle noises from above the Parlor. I sat there wondering what was going on.

India continued to sit in silence. This was now a few minutes after India had called out to Rachael asking for her a sign to show that the REM pod that went off earlier was her. On the camera's audio closest to the door, faint but heavy footsteps from down the hall began to get louder until they stopped at Rachael's door, disappearing. Three taps broke then broke out seemingly emanating from the wooden bedroom door; it was the sound of someone knocking.

India quickly turned her head in that direction. She gasped. "The door!" I think she knew that it was not me because she heard that I closed the squeaky banister door to the first floor.

"Ehh....Hello?" India cried out. The room was again silent. She turned her head towards the camera. "Someone just knocked on the door." India paused for a moment. "There's nobody out there! Rachael?" she cried out.

Maybe this is the noise that I heard from downstairs in the Parlor and was the walking in the hallway by the one that knocked on Rachael's door.

India spent another twenty minutes alone in this room before she came downstairs to inform me of her experience. At first, I had trouble believing it because I have never personally witnessed this kind of thing. But I knew India is not the kind of person to just say something without thoroughly processing it and is confident about what's being said.

I was not thinking that this was going to be as good of a piece of an experience to use in our episode until the following day while reviewing footage. The knocking was so loud and clear on the camera's audio that it could not be mistaken for being anything else. Could this of been Rachael and India had somehow established communication with her? Was she the one that seemed to be following us around the house? I needed more answers but we had many more areas of Whispers Estate to cover and it was getting late into the night.

It was only when we visited the last room around three in the morning that everything we had been experiencing all night made sense and that something terrifying took place.

CHAPTER NINE
THE WALLS THAT SCREAM

My mood at this point was better. I was starting to feel creeped out the more that I thought about the knocking. I don't recall ever feeling hyper anxious while exploring a location like I did while inside of this house. I get scared at times, of course! That is perfectly normal to be thrown off guard when looking for these kinds of things. There was just something about Whispers Estate that was affecting me. It was messing with how my mind was thinking.

After India told me about her experience with the knocking, we grabbed the cameras that were in Rachael's room and took a short break. We wanted to return to the third floor to do an EVP session in the Seance Room along with a compass. The purpose of the compass was to see if a spirit could manipulate the needle and make it move to the questions we'd ask. This would have been freaky if the needle had started to spin uncontrollably or even move on its own, but this would have been one of the coolest equipment catches.

Every location we travel to we like to try something different. A lot of the time people have no idea what we try because we do not include it in the episode. We have tried a lot of cool experiments I wish something paranormal had happened. One time we explored The Old South Pittsburgh Hospital in South Pittsburgh, Tennessee, and tried to get a spirit to give us answers we would not know.

India and I wrote one word on a piece of paper, stuck it in an envelope, and gave them to each other without saying what was inside. We then took turns in isolation in the morgue area of the hospital and used a spiritbox to ask the spirits what the piece of paper inside said without either of us opening it. This of course never worked, but this is one of the many unique things we try to do.

Our batteries were charging slowly and I just could not wait any longer. I took them off the charger and put them back into our cameras. We made our way up the stairs to the second floor. I shut the squeaky banister door behind me to seal off the sound. Everything seemed to get even quieter. Maybe I was just hyper-aware listening for any sounds that would be deemed out of place and somehow I did not notice the eeriness the last time I shut this door.

We walked around the corner and into the nursery room across from Jessie's and Rachael's room.

India stopped at the bottom of the stairs to the third floor.

"SHH." She hissed.

India thought she was hearing walking as we came around the corner into the room.

"Is somebody up there?" she cried out.

I was getting spooked. It felt like this was becoming a common occurrence for us during our entire time inside of Whispers Estate. I just felt like we were being observed and

followed around and I started to feel a subtle panic.

We paused for a moment and stared up at the black abyss that awaited us.

"Okay, here's what were going to do," India said, breaking the silence.

"We can't take too much time because I only have thirty minutes left on this camera," I interrupted.

"Okay. Let's just go," India replied.

I took each step to the third floor carefully. The wood below my feet creaked the higher I climbed.

"Hello?," I cried out as soon as the floor was in view. "Is someone up here?"

I turned to my right once I got to the final step. I ducked my head and walked through the doorway into The Seance Room and onto the step-down triangle section. India dragged her camera that was on a tripod into the room as she entered. She wanted to place her camera on the stage part of this room to face the big round table that we were going to sit at. The tripod

we were using was a cheap one and India had trouble getting it to point the right way. She struggled with it for a few moments until she called out for me to help her.

I walked up the two steps to the stage part, ducked my head, took out my cellphone to use as a flashlight, and began fixing the positioning of the camera.

"I hate these tripods," I stated.

My back was facing the four wooden studs of the wall where we could see into a room on the other side. I took a step to my left as I looked at the tripod with my flashlight. India immediately shouted out in a gasp.

"WHAT THE FUCK?"

I jumped. "Wha —"

"I just saw someone walk behind you!"

"WHAT?" I quickly turned around. I could not see anything. I started to get shivers throughout my body. We shared a moment of silence to listen for any noises.

"I literally just saw a pair of legs."

149

It took me a moment to break my shock before I responded to her.

"India, don't fuck with me."

"I'm not fucking with you. I just saw a pair of legs!"

"Okay. I don't like this place."

I turned the camera on to record.

"Come on," I firmly said to India. I wanted to start this session and get off of the third floor. I did not feel like I could be alone in any of the rooms myself even if I tried. It was like we were the ones being haunted while inside Whispers Estate. This was a new kind of experience we had never had while filming Paranormal Encounters. The atmosphere inside of this house just did not feel normal.

We sat down at the table and I wanted to question India for the camera so the audience could know what had just happened. This was because I left my main camera on the table recording when India saw the legs moving behind me.

India went on to say that this thing she saw looked like

two shadow legs moving quickly behind me and that was the best detail that she could describe. This makes sense as we were in the dark and the only light source we had was the flashlight I had on my cellphone.

"So right now, ,we are going to do an EVP session up here in the Seance Room," I began to announce to the camera. "And uh, we're going to see if we can communicate with any spirits that could reside inside of this building."

"I'm also going to be putting a compass down and see if something will spin the compass."

India sat it down on the table in front of her.

"Can you see the compass?"

"No I can't. I'll have to stand up in order to see it. Can you tilt it sideways?"

"I can't because it will mess it up," she replied.

I then stood up and told India that I could now see the compass.

"Shh. Shh," India quickly shouted. "Is somebody in

here?" she cried out. I stood still. I was terrified to look behind me. India would never know if something was there because we were in night vision and I was the only one with a camera that could see.

"Could you make a noise?" India cried out.

The room was utterly quiet. I couldn't hear a thing other than the swallowing of my spit that I did while nervously standing with my back towards where India saw those phantom legs moving.

"Can you copy me?" asked India, as she knocked three times on the table. We stood quiet for nearly a minute until I broke the silence.

"We have a device on the table right next to the compass... It has a little red light," I continued. "We can use that device to hear you. We're just going to ask you some questions. Can you tell us your name?"

I could hear two subtle clacking noises like something was moving along something.

"I hear noises back there."

Tap tap tap

These noises were not coming from the table in front of me.

"Is that you?"

India shook her head. "Who's up here?"

I zoomed my camera on the compass. It did not appear that anything was manipulating it.

"Who shut the camera off on us when we first started tonight?" I cried out asking. "That wasn't very nice."

"Where are you right now?" asked India. She paused for a moment before her next question. "Have you gone to sleep?"

We waited in silence. I saw India's eyes get huge as she looked towards me. Her mouth dropped for a moment before she could whisper to me.

"Do you hear that?"

"Yes!"

"Footsteps!"

"There's footsteps."

"Somebody's walking," added India.

We listened closely for a moment. It was like this house was still active with the ones who use to occupy it.

India lifted her right fist with one finger and pointed down. "It sounds like someone is walking around on the floor below us."

My heart began racing. "This place freaks me out, India."

"This is what we came for," she replied.

"Yeah, I know. This place is crazy."

"I think there's somebody down in that hallway. Like walking up and down."

The footsteps seemed to stop.

"Yeah....People do not understand by watching that we're in the complete dark," I said, commentating and then demonstrating what we were seeing by shutting off the night vision. "It is absolutely dark in this area," I concluded, turning the night vision back on.

"Dr. John," India cried out. "Are you here?" Her eyes stayed fixated on the doorway to the Seance Room. She could tell where I was from the little bit of light that emulated off of my camera's LCD screen.

I sat down on a chair that was behind me. I made some noise while doing this and told India that it was me. We always tag any kind of contamination from ourselves to prevent anything that could be misled into thinking something was paranormal while reviewing footage.

"Can you make a noise if you want us to leave?" India yelled out.

Two distinct knocking noises came echoing from outside the Seance Room. India quickly looked in my direction.

She whispered, "Was that you?"

"Um....I don't think so. I'm sitting still."

"I was told....That you can use your voice," India began. "Because your voices have been heard here. I've heard your voices on a recording. Why can't you talk to me now?"

India would ask me to check the compass to make sure the needle hadn't moved. It was in the same position as earlier. I told India about how freaky it was to see her in the mirror and that I could see everything behind us and our camera on a tripod.

"I want to know who's up here." India was adamant to find out who was making the footstep noises. "Can you make the loudest noise ever?"

We sat quietly for a few minutes. It was too quiet. Nothing seemed to be making any more noises.

"Alright," India said, leaning forward to press stop on our voice recorder that was sitting on the table.

Beep

"Okay. Let's go to the bathroom and do an EVP session," suggested India.

"The bathroom?"

"Yeah."

"The one where the man slipped and broke his neck?"

"Yeah, yeah."

157

"Okay." I asked India to go first and to grab the tripod on her way out.

"We have eighteen minutes left," I said, as I followed behind her, walking through the doorway to go out of the room.

"Yeah, we can do it," she confidently replied. She was sure that our camera battery had enough to last for this session. India stopped at the top of the stairs and told me to go down first since I was the one with the flashlight on my phone.

Our shoes creaked with each step that we took down to the second floor. I walked out of the nursery, turned to my right, took a few steps forward, and then took another right into the bathroom where this man died. I was a little ahead of India and I didn't realize this until I walked to the end of the bathroom and turned around. I waited for her and then asked if she could leave the camera facing us in the bathroom in between the hall and the doorway.

"Okay, it's showing the whole room."

"Okay good," I replied.

The room is very small and there was hardly enough space for us to move around. India walked into the room and decided to crawl into the bathtub while I filmed her. She got comfortable, took out the voice recorder, and hit record.

Beep

There was a sink to my right where India extended her arm to place the voice recorder. She could not see what she was doing so I grabbed it from her and placed it on the counter edge enough to keep it from falling over.

India took a deep breath and exhaled.

"Okay. I heard that there is a gentleman that passed away because he slipped and broke his neck in this bath." India paused for a moment. "If he's here,, could he tell me what his name is please?"

The bathroom was quiet. So quiet that I could hear the blood pumping in my ears. It's almost like an irritating static sound because there was nothing else that made any other noise. The bathroom also held sound because it was so narrow that

India's questions echoed. I could hear our breathing. We waited for a few moments to give enough time for a spirit to answer on the voice recorder. India continued to ask questions.

"How long were you here before someone found you?"

A few seconds after India asked this question, she thought she heard something. I wasn't sure what she was saying because most of what she said was in a whisper.

"It could of been outside, I don't know."

I looked towards our camera in the hall.

"Can you tell me, what happens when we die?" India cried out. "Do we stay here or do we go somewhere?"

We waited for a minute. I felt anxious because I was expecting to hear more footsteps, only louder. This was the area that India thought she was hearing walking while we were in the Seance Room.

"Are you stuck here?"

A noise instantly echoed into the bathroom from the hallway direction. India immediately looked towards me without

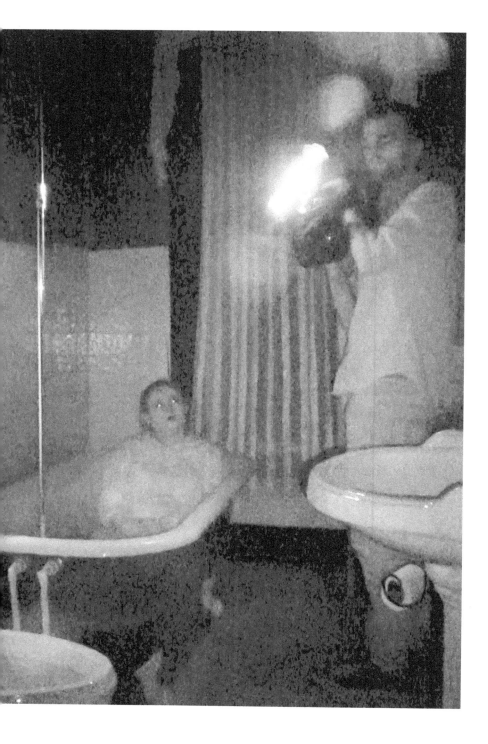

blinking and waited for this abnormal sound to stop. It lasted for five seconds.

"Did you just hear that?"

"Did you just hear a scream?" I questioned.

"YES. A scream," answered India without hesitation.

The scream echoed again into the bathroom.

"SHUSH,"

"SHH," India cried out, lifting her finger to symbolize for me to be quiet.

The scream faded abruptly. It was now subtle. It sounded like it was coming from a distance because of how loud it would get and then how faint it would go.

"It's still going," India cried out.

I whispered.

"Oh my God."

I could not believe what I was hearing. The sound was that of a child; the vocal tone of a little girl. My breathing now felt heavier. I was terrified. This was like a scream for help. But

163

where was this coming from? Did someone need our help?

We listened for a few more moments. The scream was almost not audible and then it suddenly stopped. We were trying to quickly figure out a rational explanation for this.

"I would say it would be outside but what time is it?" India asked me.

"It's," I pulled my cellphone out of my pocket to look. "Two o'clock in the morning. What kid?"

"That's what I was about to say that it sounded like a kid," India interrupted.

"What kid would be outside screaming?"

"Not Two o'clock in the morning."

"It sounds like it's in here."

"We were just outside, there's not even cars outside.

"I know. Were in a small town."

The screaming immediately came back but this time even louder. This was echoing from within the house and I was now at a loss for words. How is this even possible?

I gasped. India's mouth dropped as she pointed towards the hallway direction as we both listened to this terrifying blood-curling scream echo into our ears.

India questioned in a loud whisper.

"AGAIN?"

The screaming then faded.

India looked at me and questioned.

"Is that a scream or a frog or something?"

I turned my camera to look at the hallway.

"That's not a frog," I replied.

"There are some frogs that scream."

"Like a kid? Like a girl?"

The screaming was subtle.

"India, it sounds like a — "

"SH, India whispered.

She was trying to figure out her own conclusion about the sound. Something like this just does not happen at haunted locations; at least not for how long this was going on.

165

The scream suddenly got louder for a moment before fading quickly.

I cried out in a whisper.

"What the hell is that."

"Is it a coyote?" India questioned.

"No," I replied.

I was sure at this point that this was coming from within the walls of Whispers Estate. It was not Sondra because I was positive that this was a little girl's vocal tone. Sound should be almost impossible to hear from the first floor anyway as I had shut the banister door that leads to the first floor.

I quickly looked once again at the hallway. The screaming then disappeared as fast as when we first heard it. I paused for a moment to see if it would come back, but it didn't.

I turned to look at India. "You did ask upstairs if we could hear it. Remember?"

India was still in shock. She was still trying to figure out if this scream we thought we were hearing was some type of frog or some kind of animal.

The screaming crept back up but this time only lasted three seconds and three separate times each.

"I still hear it," India cried out. "That can't be a scream it's getting muffled."

Immediately I moved to the window to my right to satisfy any disbeliefs that India's mind was having with what was going on. I wanted to be one-hundred percent sure that nothing was happening outside even though the scream I could tell did not sound like it was coming from this direction. The window, however, had blackout tape to prevent any light from entering the home.

I turned my camera to look at the hallway once more and the horrifying noise started again. My microphone captured this scream even louder and this time was more clear that it became evident it was not outside. This is a moment that can not be replicated. I was in the full presence of a paranormal event. Was this Rachael? Was this the blood-curling scream that the

Gibbons heard when Rachael was caught in the Christmas tree fire?

Although I knew it was somewhere in the house I just could not tell from where. Each time we heard the screaming it sounded like it was moving. I took slow steps to the doorway to peek out in the hall. I wanted to see if the screaming would continue and if I could pinpoint a direction for us to follow. I slowly used my camera to look to my right towards the Servant's Quarters. The door was open halfway. I didn't see anything moving or hear any sound from that direction.

I then looked to my left towards Rachael's Room. I realized the screaming had stopped before I got to the doorway. It was gone and would return no more. I turned around and walked back to where I was standing.

"I don't know where it's at. That hallways really freaky. It's two o'clock in the morning. It's defiantly not a kid outside."

"I'm not saying it's not a kid. We just haven't heard it any other time."

169

"We have ten minutes left on this battery."

India paused for a moment. "Okay. Let's go downstairs."

"Okay. Stopping the recording,," I replied. I picked up the voice recorder and stopped the recording. I helped India out of the bathtub and we grabbed our things and went downstairs. This was the last thing we did at Whispers Estate. The scream took everything out of us. My mind was racing a million times faster than normal because I was trying to understand what I just heard. Was it Rachael? I think at the moment that it was happening we had no idea what to think or who to assume it was.

It was getting close to three in the morning at this point. We only had the place till four and this was not enough time to charge our camera batteries to continue on and so we decided to pack up our things and load them into my car for the trip back to the hotel. It would be only a few hours I would get that night because the terrifying sound still echoed in my head. It still does to this very day. I think about this often.

———— ⁙⧉◆❍◗◕❍⧉⁙ ————

I have not been to a location since that has left my mind in an entanglement as much as Whispers Estate has done to me. I feel drawn to this house. I feel attached to the experiences that I had this night.

I walked through the front door of Whispers Estate and got everything I asked for and more. I experienced something significant in the realm of the paranormal for I cannot get over it. These are moments that the veil of a different plane of existence someone bleeds through to our own. It is the same type of event that happened when I witnessed the only ghost I've ever seen when I first went seeking these kinds of things.

I was told that this haunted location in the small town of Mitchell, Indiana, was known for its whispers, but instead, it is known only to me as the walls that scream.

CHAPTER TEN
DEATH | PART II

Death. That word alone carries depression, fear, and sorrowfulness all at once. I can not think of a more devastating word to share with someone who is affected by this.

When I think of death I think of the inability to share memories. The phone calls and text messages cease, and that one-of-kind energy a person is so fond of — dissipates. It is a barrier; at least for some.

Does that mean that death is the end? The point where everything becomes black and the realization of being alive is no longer a conscious thought or process for survival. Emptiness. The great abyss.

Survival. Why do we fight so hard to be alive? Even paranormal investigators have this same reaction and instinct.

Why is that? Some have already seen a ghost or had their life-long fill of answers they needed, or so they thought they needed. Maybe it's just closure they were seeking from the weight of the pain they've carried for far too long.

I saw a movie once that was highly thought-provoking. There aren't many supernatural movies I take anything from but this one struck a chord. It's called *The Discovery*. It's about a scientist who discovers proof of an afterlife. He went looking for this because of his guilt from the loss of his wife and he wanted to make sure that she made it somewhere after her death. The scientist finds proof that the consciousness of a person moves to a different plane of existence after one dies. He was able to show the world this said proof and once people found value in this new scientific discovery, the suicide rate skyrockets.

It got me thinking that if we truly knew that there was some type of life beyond death, would that change anything? Would there be a mass suicide rate too? The reasoning behind this is rather simple. Why would a person want to stay on Earth and suffer, be in debt, be cheated on, lose a pet, or a loved one at any moment without warning? What if we could just make it all go away and have utter bliss and a restart of our existence?

I believe it's because regardless of what people say when one claims they know there is an afterlife — they still fear death; we all do. It's the fear of letting go and accepting that you're not the one in control. It also comes down to our basic human instinct of survival.

I have been fortunate enough to not have so much death around while growing up, but I still hold on to the hurt of the ones that I did lose along the way to my thirty years of living. The feeling never goes away, it just hides behind a corner and waits to pop out when I least expect it. There is no real closure with death. Our mind sees patterns of familiarity from things we encounter and relates them to the personality of the ones lost. This creates grief. What is it about the person's personality that creates this pull towards them? Even though the one we miss is physically gone from Earth, could we still consciously communicate with them in some way?

My time at Whispers Estate is still one of my greatest paranormal explorations. I cannot wrap my mind around the footsteps, the knocking, and the screaming. How are these types of phenomenon even possible? Like the scientist from The Discovery, does a piece of our conscious stay in this plane of existence, only separated from the physical form? Maybe this can explain phantom footsteps, knocking, and screaming. I have to ponder how it would be possible to communicate verbally without vocal cords if one is a ghost. Maybe our idea of how the human body works is merely an illusion and the vocal tones are not entirely from the physical form. I wonder these things because every paranormal experience I have been gifted to witness, I take pride with. This is because I do not believe any of it can ever be replicated as every encounter is unique in its own way.

India and I have been to numerous places that the public is unaware of. We just have never talked about them because nothing was captured or not enough was captured to even call it paranormal. Maybe the paranormal community should start sharing all the times of nothingness. That might create a sense of value in what's being shown and not the fabricated entitlement that unexplainable things happen often.

Most people are too caught up trying to get on television for attention that deep down, it was never about the paranormal in the first place. This field is just the easiest to fake and sadly, there are too many people good at it. I find that no matter what is presented, people become so conditioned that they will always expect more — the next big scariest thing.

Everything that I share with the public is valued evidence that I have tried to explain away, but could not replicate and I look at it as authentic. The paranormal is rare. It is witnessed less than one is to believe. Any person who goes into a foreign building can hear noises or think they see something. The building is settling, animals, carbon monoxide poisoning, mold, you name it. That makes it easy to claim something is paranormal. If a group or show provides paranormal evidence as a common thing, one should be wary.

Every time I go to write more to this book, it puts me in a dark space. I have to fully give in to it. I have to embrace this. I need it to fully express my conscious thoughts and to get my message across. The only way that someone can learn is by submerging into it and having empathy for what's not theirs.

I still remember every detail of the day when I saw a ghost, and to this day, the only ghost that I've seen. This experience was only seconds, but the vivid details remain. When this type of phenomenon happens, a person just has this intuitiveness to know that this is real and the mind tries to make sense of it with what's been taught in the physical world. I can capture audio recordings and see lights go off on paranormal equipment all night but nothing is made or prepares a person to understand what one sees when a spirit is physically and clearly seen without the need for additives, equipment, or hallucinogenics. Despite witnessing the holy grail of my human existence — *The*

Discovery. I do not feel any closure on death in the slightest bit. It is the thief in the night who steals without thought. Every day that I breathe air on Earth is another year, month, day, hour, minute, and second closer that I am to death.

This book is not your proof of life after death. My words, my books, my show, or any of the paranormal shows for that matter should not be any form of proof or closure to one's feelings. It's weird to say but I feel more alive when I go on supernatural adventures. I seek to experience rather than seek attention. I record them because I want to relive my rare moments of paranormal encounters. I share them because I want the world to witness authentic phenomenon without all the fluff, and to validate that they're not alone nor crazy.

The story of Rachael and the ghost stories behind Whispers Estate is still considered legend and lore without any factual documentation to back up the claims. However, something is inside this quiet white house that sits in the small town of Mitchell, Indiana. I can say that with certainty as I now understand why this is called one of America's most terrifying places. I hear this ringing inside my head that I can not seem to shake. I have heard *the walls that scream.*

ABOUT THE AUTHOR

CONNOR **BIDDLE** is an American documentary filmmaker who has been creating films since 2010 based on the paranormal. He had his first paranormal experience as a child in a home he grow up in that was built in 1862.

Since then throughout his years in high school his interest in the paranormal only grew when he visited Waverly Hills Sanatorium in 2010 with a couple of friends. During a tour of the building he captured voices on a audio recorder that he couldn't explain. In 2012 he set out to film a documentary which he is known for called Paranormal Encounters: A Haunting at Farrar Elementary. Being skeptical at first when arriving Connor began having experiences throughout his investigation that led him continue traveling to reportedly haunted locations.

Connor continues filming a series called Paranormal Encounters in which he is the executive producer and co-host along side with his fiancé India.

LISTEN TO THE ENTIRE VOICE RECORDING OF THE SCREAM WE CAPTURED IN THE BATHROOM ON THE SECOND FLOOR OF WHISPERS ESTATE.

WATCH

PARANORMAL ENCOUNTERS

CPSIA information can be obtained
at www.ICGtesting.com
Printed in the USA
BVHW040754100522
636621BV00001B/17

9 780578 397191